THE G.I. SERIES

The War in Korea
Korea
The U.S. Army in Korea, 1950–1953

Gunner Robert Oserstrat (left) and Private First Class (PFC) Ray Wyatt (right) fire high explosive (HE) shells from their 4.2-inch chemical mortar, which was also used for smoke shells. It had originally been developed for gas shells.

THE G.I. SERIES

THE ILLUSTRATED HISTORY OF THE AMERICAN SOLDIER, HIS UNIFORM AND HIS EQUIPMENT

The War in Korea
The U.S. Army in Korea, 1950–1953

Christopher J. Anderson

Greenhill Books
LONDON

Stackpole Books
PENNSYLVANIA

Greenhill Books

This book is humbly dedicated to all the members of the United Nations forces who served in Korea, and specifically to Albert Howse.

The War in Korea
first published 2001 by Greenhill Books, Lionel Leventhal Limited, Park House, 1 Russell Gardens, London NW11 9NN
www.greenhillbooks.com
and
Stackpole Books, 5067 Ritter Road, Mechanicsburg, PA 17055, USA

British Library Cataloguing in Publication Data
Anderson, Christopher J.
The war in Korea : the U.S. Army in Korea, 1950-1953. - (The G.I. series : the illustrated history of the American soldier, his uniform and his equipment ; v. 23)
1. United States. Army - Uniforms 2. United States. Army - History 3. Korean War, 1950-1953
I. Title
951.9'042

ISBN 1-85367-443-5

Library of Congress Cataloging-in-Publication Data
Anderson, Christopher J.
The war in Korea : The U.S. Army in Korea, 1950-1953 / Christopher J. Anderson.
    p.   cm. — (The G.I. series ; v 23)
Includes bibliographical references.

ISBN 1-85367-443-5
1. Korean War, 1950-1953—United States—Pictorial works. 2. United States. Army—History—Korean War, 1950-1953—Pictorial works. 3. United States. Army—Uniforms—History—20th century—Pictorial works. 4. United States. Army—Equipment—History—20th century—Pictorial works. I. Title. II. Series.
DS919.A64 2001
951.904'24—dc21   00-067020

Visit www.greenhillbooks.com and access the Cumulative Index to the G.I. Series
More than 2,000 images have been published in the G.I. Series, creating one of the most extensive collections of images of the American soldier ever assembled and available to the public. The unique reference index, which can be easily accessed through the Greenhill website, serves as a precise guide to this wealth of images in the series.

All photographs in this book are courtesy of the U.S. Army.

Front cover illustration: Two members of the 35th Regimental Combat Team scan the horizon for enemy troop movement in August 1950. They are wearing World War II era fatigue uniforms and carrying Mk II fragmentation grenades, bandoliers of ammunition and M1 Garand rifles.

Designed by David Gibbons, DAG Publications Ltd
Layout by Anthony A. Evans, DAG Publications Ltd
Printed in Hong Kong

THE WAR IN KOREA
THE U.S. ARMY IN KOREA, 1950–1953

In the five years after World War II, the energy of the American public was fixed firmly on domestic matters and a booming economy. Little attention was paid to the fact that the U.S. armed forces had shrunk from a high of twelve million in 1945 to a mere 1.5 million men and women. With much of the rest of the world prostrate and trying to recover from the destruction of the world war, this tiny force was deemed sufficient by the Truman administration to meet the army's constabulary obligations in the occupied zones of America's former enemies as well as to provide for national defense. Many believed that efforts to contain Communism could be largely confined to diplomacy, the threat of nuclear retaliation, or through financial aid to countries faced with a Communist threat.

One place where the struggle against Communist expansion was being played out was Korea, which had been a colony of the Japanese Empire for the first half of the twentieth century. To prevent all of Korea from falling under Soviet control in 1945, American officials proposed that the country be divided into two zones of occupation separated by the 38th Parallel. Josef Stalin agreed to this proposal, and in September 1945, American forces arrived in South Korea.

After the war, efforts by the former allies to agree a solution to the question of Korean independence failed and in the spring of 1948 the United Nations proposed that the citizens of the peninsula would elect a national assembly for the country. South of the 38th Parallel, this election resulted in the ratification of a constitution for the Republic of Korea (ROK) and the election of Korean nationalist Dr. Syngman Rhee to the presidency. In the north, however, Soviet authorities prevented the UN mandated election from taking place, and held separate elections in the fall of 1948 that led to the appointment of Kim Il Sung as the president of the newly created Democratic People's Republic of Korea.

With the establishment of an independent republic on the Korean Peninsula, albeit one that only included territory below the 38th Parallel, Washington believed that its occupation duties had ended and withdrew the bulk of its forces. By the summer of 1949, the only American military personnel who remained in Korea were the 500 members of the Korean Military Advisory Group (KMAG). KMAG was tasked with training ROK military personnel. However, while the Soviet Union provided Kim Il Sung with large numbers of T-34 tanks and heavy artillery, the newly created ROK Army was envisioned as being little more than a police force and was equipped with only small arms and a few light artillery pieces. Believing that the United States would not intervene in a bid to unify the peninsula under Kim Il Sung, Communist leaders began to prepare for military intervention.

At 4 a.m. on the morning of June 25, 1950, North Korean artillery batteries saturated ROK positions south of the 38th Parallel. Shortly after the first artillery rounds flew across the border, 90,000 North Korean soldiers, many of them veterans of the recently concluded civil war in China, supported by 150 Soviet built T-34 tanks, crashed across the border in the direction of Seoul, the ROK capital.

When word of the North Korean attack reached the United States, President Harry S. Truman immediately authorized General Douglas MacArthur, the commander of America's forces in the Far East, to provide what assistance he could to the beleaguered South Korean army. Fearing that U.S. popular opinion would not support American involvement in another war, Truman maintained that this was only a 'Police Action.' Meanwhile, the UN Security Council called for an end to the invasion by North Korea, and, when this was ignored, it passed a resolution calling for international cooperation in defense of South Korea. Although not every UN country sent military forces, many eventually did, including Canada,

Great Britain, France, Turkey, Australia, Belgium and Norway. Although the numbers never approached those committed by the United States, the presence of troops from a variety of countries was a valuable indication of UN resolve. Despite the UN's actions, however, the North Korean forces seized Seoul and continued to advance south.

The nearest UN troops were the four critically under equipped and under strength American divisions serving on occupation duty in Japan. On June 30, President Truman authorized General MacArthur to commit U.S. ground forces to Korea. MacArthur believed that the mere presence of G.I.s on the peninsula would cause the North Koreans to lose heart and halt their advance, and instructed Major General Walton Walker, the Eighth Corps commander, to transport the 24th Infantry Division to South Korea as soon as possible. To encourage the South Koreans and provide a show of strength, Walker assembled an improvised battalion from the ranks of the 24th Infantry Division and flew them to Korea. On July 2, the 400 men of Task Force Smith (named after their commander Lieutenant Colonel Charles B. Smith) arrived in Korea and were rushed to the front near Osan with orders to block the main road to the vital port of Pusan.

Task Force Smith was inadequately armed and equipped and, on July 5, unable to stop a large force of North Korean tanks from overrunning their positions. Although Smith's command resisted briefly, Communist tanks and soldiers crushed the tiny U.S. force and killed and captured more than half its number. All that Task Force Smith had accomplished was to illustrate graphically how unprepared the Army was to fight a war against a well-equipped and determined foe.

Three of the four U.S. divisions in Japan were badly under their authorized strength and their regiments only had two of the authorized three battalions. In addition, the divisions lacked artillery and armored forces. Little money had been expended on new equipment and ammunition (in Japan there were fewer than twenty rounds of anti-tank shells available) and most of what was available included stocks of materiel that had been in storage since 1945. Lieutenant General Mathew B. Ridgway later recalled, 'We were, in short, in a state of shameful unreadiness.'

Throughout July the remainder of the 24th Infantry Division fought a series of desperate delaying actions against Communist forces while Generals Walker and MacArthur struggled to get additional UN forces to Korea (MacArthur had been named overall commander of UN forces on July 7). On the 22nd, the newly arrived 1st Cavalry Division relieved the remnants of the 24th Infantry Division. Although the sacrifice of the 24th Infantry Division had provided MacArthur with the time he needed to rush reinforcements to Korea, at the end of July it still looked as though the UN would be permanently kicked off the peninsula.

By August, all that remained in the hands of UN forces was a tiny perimeter around Pusan on the southeast coast of Korea. If Pusan fell, Kim Il Sung's dream of reuniting Korea would have been realized. Walker had managed to assemble 45,000 U.S. troops. There were also 45,000 ROK troops, almost all that remained of the ROK army, within the perimeter as well. Opposing Walker were 70,000 North Korean troops. Although Walker outnumbered his opponent, his troops had been roughly handled during the previous month and Kim Il Sung's men were flush with victory.

Throughout August the North Koreans launched repeated assaults along the perimeter that achieved limited breakthroughs but were beaten back with the assistance of airpower. On September 2 they launched their final offensives along the perimeter, pushing six miles closer to Pusan before their advance was eventually halted. The UN forces (contingents from the UK had arrived from Hong Kong on September 29) had been able to retain a toehold in Korea.

MacArthur knew that he could never restore Syngman Rhee to power he forces continued to retreat in the face of North Korean advances. Even while Walker's men were battling for their lives around Pusan, MacArthur was making plans to change the course of the war and regain the initiative. In what many consider to be the most brilliant operation of his military career, MacArthur planned to land the few troops remaining to him (one Marine and one Army Division) at Inchon, a port on the coast 25 miles west of Seoul, while General Walker's forces went on the counterattack around Pusan. Many people, citing the desperate situation around Pusan and the hazardous tides at Inchon, encouraged MacArthur to consider a landing elsewhere. Undaunted, MacArthur insisted on carrying out the operation as planned. The general realized that the North Korean forces had been battering themselves against the Pusan perimeter and were operating at the end of a long supply line. By landing at Inchon, MacArthur hoped to recapture the South Korean capital and then advance across the peninsula, thereby trapping the overextended North Korean army.

On September 15, the Inchon landings, codenamed Operation Chromite, began. By the evening of the 15th, the Marines had landed, seized

Inchon, and begun to advance inland. The next day, the Army's 7th Infantry Division had landed and, along with the Marines, were advancing toward Seoul. Meanwhile, on the 16th, Walker began his breakout from the Pusan perimeter. Soon, the North Korean army, caught between Walker and MacArthur, was disintegrating under the blows of resurgent UN forces. On the 19th Seoul was reached and for the next ten days Marines and G.I.s fought a brutal street battle to regain control of the ROK capital. On September 29, with the remnants of some Communist units still battling amidst the ruins, General MacArthur officially turned control of the capital city over to President Syngman Rhee.

President Truman then authorized MacArthur, in early October, to cross the 38th Parallel and continue the UN advance into North Korea, while North Korean forces struggled to regroup. The disintegration of Kim Il Sung's forces was now causing alarm in Beijing and Moscow, and to prevent their defeat, Chinese troops crossed the Yalu River into North Korea on October 13. What had begun as a dispute over control of a small Asian country now threatened to escalate into another world war. Despite the threat of a clash with the Chinese, Truman hoped that UN forces would be able to secure total victory and reunite Korea before the Communists could recover. On October 19, when UN forces seized the North Korean capital of Pyongyang, it appeared that Truman's wish would be granted.

So elated were they by their success, that MacArthur, Walker, and many other UN officers refused to credit the increasing number of reports that announced the presence of large numbers of Chinese Communist troops entering Korea even after Chinese troops battered a ROK division. American officers refused to believe that they were faced with a new strategic situation. However, even sceptical American intelligence officers were forced to face reality when, on November 1, elements of the 1st Cavalry Division found themselves engaged in a fierce battle with Chinese Communist soldiers. Fighting against Chinese forces continued until the 6th when, unexpectedly, calm settled over the front.

MacArthur mistakenly believed that the lull indicated that the Chinese had withdrawn back across the border and ordered the Eighth Corps and Tenth Corps to continue their advance. Despite the unsettling presence of Chinese forces and the first chilling indications of how cold a Korean winter could be, many in the UN command believed that they were in on the end of the war and the 'home by Christmas' rumor was heard on the lips of many of the soldiers.

Plans for enjoying the holidays with loved ones came to an abrupt end on November 27 when the Chinese launched a massive counteroffensive. Soon UN forces were reeling under the attacks of waves of Chinese Communist forces. All along the front UN forces began a fighting withdrawal and MacArthur, who had chosen to ignore the presence of 300,000 Chinese troops now had to announce, 'We face an entirely new war.'

Throughout the end of November and in to December, as weather conditions steadily worsened, UN forces fought a series of desperate delaying actions as they sought to avoid being totally overwhelmed. UN contingents frequently found themselves surrounded by Communist troops and forced to fight their way out of encirclement. Efforts to halt the Communist advance proved fruitless and by December 5 the Eighth Army abandoned Pyongyang and retreated to the 38th Parallel. Although many men were able to escape, casualties among the battered divisions of the Eighth Corps were heavy. Among those killed during the chaotic retreat was the corps commander, General Walker.

In the east, the Tenth Corps retreat included the epic withdrawal of the 1st Marine Division and elements of the Army's 7th Infantry Division from the Chosin Reservoir. Finally, after a running battle against Chinese Communist forces in positions in the hills along their route, the survivors of the Chosin Reservoir reached safety. Once the Tenth Corps remnants had reached Hungnam, they were evacuated south to Pusan.

The end of 1950 saw UN forces in a state of disarray. The day after Christmas, Lieutenant General Mathew B. Ridgway arrived to replace Walker and attempt to restore the situation. Less than a week after arriving at his new command, Ridgway was forced to contain the Chinese New Year's Offensive. Still reeling from the loss of General Walker and the retreat from the Yalu, UN forces were unable to halt the Chinese advance and, on January 4, 1951, Seoul was again abandoned to the Communists. UN forces were unable to halt the enemy advance until reaching the 37th Parallel. There, more due to lengthening supply lines than UN opposition, the Chinese advance came to a halt.

Given a temporary respite, Ridgway used this time to repair his command's badly shaken morale and to prepare to return to the offensive. On January 25, Ridgway launched Operation Thunderbolt, which was followed by Operations Killer and Ripper. Throughout the remaining winter months, UN forces took advantage of shortened supply lines, airpower and armor to halt the final Communist advances. During these counteroffensives Ridgway used superior firepower to destroy enemy formations rather than continue the seesaw effort to seize and hold terrain. Slowly, these offensives began to gain momentum and drive the enemy back past the territory they had gained during their New Year's Offensive. Ridgway's counteroffensives culminated with the liberation of Seoul for the second time on March 18.

Many blamed the disastrous final months of 1950 on MacArthur and saw Ridgway as the man who had saved the situation. MacArthur's relations with Truman were at an all time low, and with the situation in Korea stabilized, on April 11, in one of the most controversial decisions of his administration, the president relieved MacArthur and replaced him with Ridgway. Lieutenant General James A. Van Fleet was selected to replace Ridgway as commander of the Eighth U.S. Army in Korea.

The Eighth Army's new commander had only been with his command for a short time when, on May 10, Communist forces began a renewed offensive to take Seoul. Having regained confidence in their abilities, UN troops were able to inflict serious causalities on Communist forces as they battered themselves against their positions. By the end of the month, the Communist drive had been stopped and Eighth Army soldiers renewed attacks intended to destroy what enemy troops remained below the 38th Parallel.

The conflict in Korea had, again, reached a stalemate. On June 23rd Jacob Malik, the Russian delegate to the UN, proposed a truce along the line that was currently held and, on July 10, truce talks began at Kaesong. Both sides agreed, however, that hostilities would continue until a final armistice was signed. The war now entered, perhaps, one of its oddest phases. While negotiators engaged in continuous talks, the Communist and UN troops continued to fight each other in a series of small, but often brutal, battles. The front lines, formerly very fluid, now became fixed with both sides digging in and creating elaborate defensive positions more reminiscent of World War I.

For the next two years, while negotiations continued at Kaesong, and later Panmunjon, both sided fought a series of battles at obscure hills to obtain the most advantageous position prior to a negotiated settlement. Finally, after 37 months of fighting, on July 27, 1953, a truce was signed and the fighting stopped. The final truce line was along the 38th Parallel and was largely unchanged from what it had been when North Korean forces had first crossed the border in June 1950. Unwilling to accept the permanent division of his country, Republic of Korea President Syngman Rhee refused to sign a peace treaty with North Korea and the two Koreas remain, to this day, still technically at war with one another. Friendly gestures in 2000 may develop into a lasting rapprochement, or not.

Although they had been thrust unprepared into the first great struggle of the Cold War, the American servicemen and women who were sent to Korea fought doggedly to secure the freedom of the Republic of Korea and to halt the spread of Communism. Of all the U.S. armed services that fought in Korea, none paid a higher price than the U.S. Army. More than 27,000 G.I.s were killed in Korea and another 77,000 wounded. Despite their losses, however, the role of the G.I.s in what has become known as 'The Forgotten War' has, until only recently, been neglected. It is hoped that now, after more than fifty years, the sacrifices of all of the men and women who participated in the first furious shots of the Cold War will finally be remembered.

For Further Reading

Dvorchak, Robert J., *The Battle For Korea: The Associated Press History of the Korean Conflict* (Combined Publishing, 1993, 50th anniversary edition, 2000).

Hogg, Ian V. (ed), *The American Arsenal: The World War II Official Standard Ordnance Catalog* (Greenhill Books, 1996).

Lewis, Kenneth, *Doughboy to G.I.: U.S. Army Clothing and Equipment 1900-1945* (Norman D. Landing Publishing, 1993).

Sandler, Stanley (ed.), *The Korean War: An Encyclopedia* (Garland Publishing, 1995).

Stanton, Shelby, *U.S. Army Uniforms of the Korean War* (Stackpole Books, 1992).

Stokesbury, James L., *A Short History of the Korean War* (Quill, 1988).

U.S. Department of Defense, Korean War Fact Sheets (various).

Above: Members of the 674th Field Artillery Battalion, attached to the 187th Regimental Combat Team (RCT) (Airborne), fire their 105mm howitzer at Chinese positions. The men are all wearing M50 field jackets, almost identical to the earlier M43 field jacket, and M51 trousers, similar to M43 field trousers, but with a pleated patch pocket sewn to each thigh.

Right: Private First Class (PFC) Charles E. Tisdale from the 25th Infantry Division stands by his M1917A1 .30-caliber Browning machine gun. A can containing 250 rounds of belted ammunition rests on a shelf affixed to the side of the gun. The red-tipped rounds signify tracer ammunition, which would be used to sight the weapon during firing; the black-tip rounds are armor piercing.

Left: A heavy mortar platoon of the 25th Infantry Division fires on enemy positions in the Mung Dung-Ni Valley. All of these men are wearing M1 steel helmets for ballistic protection while firing their 4.2-inch chemical mortar. The mortarman second from the right has painted rank insignia (sergeant's) to the front of his helmet. This practice was far more common during the Korean War than it had been during World War II.

Below: The crew of a 90mm artillery piece fire on enemy positions. The men are all wearing herringbone twill (HBT) fatigue uniforms, with the jackets tucked into the trousers, as was the fashion after World War II.

Artillerymen fire their 90mm gun from its fixed position, which is sheltered behind a wall of sandbags, and concealed with camouflage netting. The gunner kneeling at the left receives firing coordinates through the headset underneath his helmet.

Above: A Sikorski H-4 helicopter delivers casualties to the 8055 Mobile Army Surgical Hospital (MASH). Korea was the first war in which helicopters saw extensive service and their use as airborne ambulances often proved the difference between life and death for wounded GIs.

Left: A mortar crew prepares to fire a round from its 81mm mortar. While the gunner at right sights the piece, the crewman at left prepares to drop a round down the tube. The gunner has a regimental insignia attached to the side of his highly polished helmet liner, indicating that this photograph was either staged, or taken during a training exercise.

A Browning Automatic Rifle (BAR) gunner shelters behind a wall. First developed during World War I, the BAR was widely used throughout World War II and the Korean War. This soldier supports his M1937 rifleman's belt with M1945 combat suspenders, which were wider in the shoulder than the earlier M1936 suspenders. During the Korean War, the use of web equipment from a variety of model years was common.

Left: General Mathew B. Ridgway sits for his official photograph in the spring of 1951, shortly after replacing General Douglas MacArthur as commander of all United Nations forces in Korea. He is wearing the wool elastique service coat with khaki shirt and tie. By this time, the elastique coat was considered semi-dress and was being replaced by the short wool serge service jacket. On the left breast of his jacket are his medal ribbons, which bear witness to his distinguished service in World War II: there are so many that they extend onto the pocket flap. His jumpwings above the ribbons bear a small star, signifying a combat jump, in this case his jump into Normandy with the 82nd Airborne Division on June 6, 1944.

Top right: Two members of the 187th RCT rush past a burning village north of Tanyang, Korea. They are wearing field jackets and trousers with pile field caps. The pile cap was extremely popular in Korea. The field jacket and trousers were constructed of heavyweight cotton and were intended to be worn over additional layers of clothing.

Right: A South Korean officer briefs his men while an American advisor, with blue and white X Corps insignia on his jacket, looks on. All of the Korean soldiers are armed, equipped and clothed entirely in American supplied items. The soldiers are all carrying M1 Garand rifles and are wearing M43 pattern webbing equipment, which can be identified by its darker Olive Drab (OD) Number 7 shade. The .30-caliber Garand, which entered service just before World War II, remained the GI's standard service rifle during the Korean War.

Right: General Douglas MacArthur (right), in command of a multi-national force, discusses the military situation with two French officers. France supplied units that were attached to the U.S. 2d Infantry Division. The officer on the left is wearing a brand new field jacket, while the officer in the center is wearing a cotton fatigue uniform over a sweater and wool shirt. MacArthur wears a privately purchased pile-lined parka with his famous embroidered khaki service cap.

Right: Reporters surround representatives of the United Nations as they arrive in Panmunjon for the final armistice discussions. The two officials on the left are wearing HBT fatigue uniforms, while the air force officer in the doorway of the helicopter is wearing an army issue khaki cotton shirt and trousers with an air force service cap.

Above: Members of the 2d Infantry Division prepare to fire their .30-caliber M1919A6 light machine gun at Communist forces in October 1950. The M1919A6, like most of the weapons used by G.I.s during the Korean War, was a holdover from World War II.

Below: The last elements of the 7th Regimental Combat Team (RCT), 3d Infantry Division, complete their evacuation from Hungnam, Korea, on Christmas Eve, 1950. These men are driving a WC52 Dodge weapons carrier with 1-ton trailer.

Above: A group of G.I.s relax after a patrol. The men are wearing a combination of early World War II olive drab (OD) shade 9 and late war OD shade 7 web gear. The OD7 equipment first became available in the later stages of World War II and large stocks remained at the end of the war. The soldier with his back to the camera has stenciled his name and home state on the back of his fatigue jacket.

Below: Members of the 27th Infantry Regiment, 25th Infantry Division, follow a tank into an area on the Wasan front that has been infiltrated by North Korean soldiers. This squad of G.I.s is lightly equipped, carrying only canteens, entrenching tools and ammunition. The man marching at the rear is armed with a Browning Automatic Rifle (BAR), the squad's automatic weapon.

Right: Soldiers of the 7th Infantry Division on a road march at Camp Fuji, Japan, in August 1950. The years of occupation duty in Japan meant that many of the G.I.s first sent to Korea were ill prepared for the rigors of combat operations. After the war began, however, soldiers in Japan were put through a crash course of physical training. These men are all wearing herringbone twill (HBT) utility uniforms. They have improvised helmet covers from burlap.

Below: Prentiss Thrower uses his water-cooled M1917A1 .30-caliber machine gun against North Korean forces near Taegu in the summer of 1950. The A1, an effective weapon, was extremely heavy (93 lb when mounted on its tripod) and generally only suited for use in fixed positions.

Above: A chemical mortar crew fires on advancing Communist forces. All of these men are wearing HBT uniforms left over from World War II. The officer standing on the right has pinned a pair of crossed rifles, signifying his branch of service, to his left collar.

Below: After fifteen days on the line, members of the 5th RCT are being taken in a GMC CCKW 2½ ton truck to the rear for a rest. The famous 'deuce and a half' was the workhorse of the American army, as it had been in World War II.

Below: During the retreat in the winter of 1950 three members of the 65th Engineers work to destroy a bridge north of Sairwon, North Korea, in an effort to slow the advance of Communist troops. The three men are wearing a variety of cold weather clothing including (center) an M1942 enlisted man's overcoat.

Above: The crew members of a heavy mortar cover their ears against the sound of the gun's blast. The soldier at right cradles another round for his weapon in his lap. He has attached his wristwatch through a buttonhole on the lapel of his fatigue jacket, to prevent it being damaged while firing.

Above: A wire team from the 24th Infantry Division repairs a telephone line that has been cut during action near Pongdong, Korea. All four men are wearing the M43 field jacket. First introduced during World War II, the versatile M43 field jacket, and the improved M1950 model, were the most frequently worn jackets of the Korean conflict.

Below: Members of the 7th Infantry Division assemble on the beach at Iwon, Korea, while their equipment is unloaded from LST QO73. The frequent amphibious operations of the Korean War relied heavily on the LST, which had seen extensive service in World War II.

Above: Members of the 65th RCT work with Republic of Korea (ROK) troops to destroy rolling stock before the arrival of Communist forces. The variety of parkas, field jackets and field overcoats reflects the rather haphazard nature of supply early in the war. Most of these men are wearing the detachable hood from the M1943 field jacket for additional warmth.

Below: Soldiers of the 1st battalion, 19th Infantry Regiment, 24th Infantry Division, relax after crossing the Naktong River in September 1950 during the breakout from the Pusan perimeter. Per regulation, the jeep at the right of the picture has the unit's designation painted on the bumper.

Above: Brigadier General Henry Hodes, assistant commander of the 7th Infantry Division (in the jeep), confers with an officer from the 17th Infantry Regiment during the fighting for Seoul in September 1950. The officer at left has taken a piece of camouflaged parachute material and fashioned a helmet cover, which he wears under a loose mesh net.

Below: An M2A-1 105mm howitzer from the 25th Infantry Division is towed across an improvised bridge during the breakout from the Pusan perimeter. This was the primary artillery piece of all United Nations forces during the Korean War. The howitzer's crew of eight men could fire up to eight rounds per minute at targets more than 11 kilometers away.

Above: Men of the 32d Infantry Regiment, 7th Infantry Division, advance to the front lines in September 1950. All wear cotton fatigues. Several at the rear of the column have draped M2 ammunition carriers over their shoulders and carry additional rounds for the unit's M18 recoilless rifle, which is visible in the middle of the column.

Below: During the bitter street fighting in Seoul in September 1950, the commander of A company, 32d Infantry, consults his map and radios headquarters for further instructions. Standing behind the officer is the company commander's radioman, carrying an SCR-300/BC 1000 man-pack radio, which was standard issue to all infantry platoons.

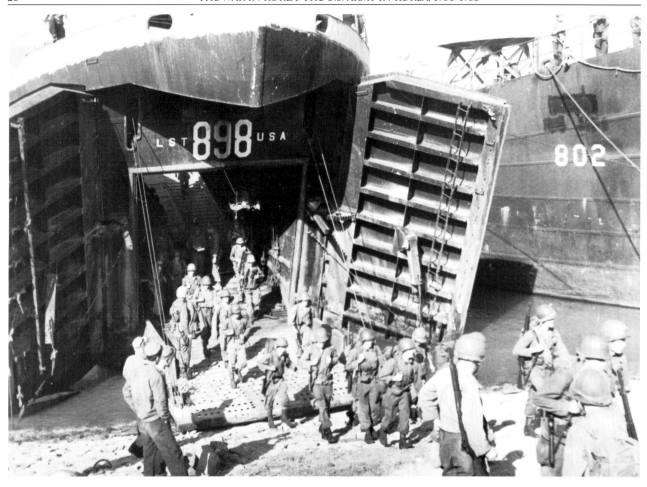

Above: Infantrymen disembark from an LST. All are wearing the cotton fatigue uniform. The man standing fifth from right with his back to the camera has a newly issued pair of trousers and a well-worn jacket. The color variation between the jacket and trousers illustrates how much these garments would fade with wear.

Left: PFC Wilbert E. Perkins receives a fire order while Corporal Harold Wynne records the information. Both men wear World War II fatigues. Perkins is also wearing the early pattern HBT mechanic's cap, which had a shortened bill.

Right: A group of G.I.s proudly displays a variety of captured Communist weapons. The man at center is wearing what appears to be an M1941 HBT 'Daisy Mae' fatigue hat. This was obsolete by the end of World War II and its use by a soldier in Korea would be unique. The G.I. directly in front of him has a pair of M1944 plastic goggles around his neck.

Below: General Lawton Collins (front seat) and Lieutenant General Mathew B. Ridgway (back seat) greet Colonel William Harris during an inspection in January 1951. Colonel Harris is wearing a World War II reversible ski parka. He has attached a 3d Infantry Division insignia to his left shoulder and regimental insignia on a green combat commander's identification tab on his epaulettes.

Opposite page, top: Tanks of the 1st Cavalry Division cover infantrymen as they advance on Communist forces. Tanks frequently provided fire support for advancing infantry units. While the tank's guns lob 76 mm shells at the enemy, the commander of the tank at right stands on the rear deck of his Sherman to fire his vehicle's .50-caliber machine gun.

Above: Members of the 3d Infantry Division, wearing field jackets with pile field caps, return from a combat patrol. Several of them have slung extra bandoliers of .30-caliber ammunition over their shoulders. The loose formation of this patrol indicates that it is still close to the enemy.

Left: Members of the 15th RCT, 3d Infantry Division, pose in front of a tank after receiving the bronze star medal. Several of the men are wearing the pile field jacket while others wear the M43 field jacket. The pile jacket was developed during World War II and was originally intended to be worn under the M43, but in Korea was often worn separately. In addition to their bronze star medals, several of these men proudly display their combat infantry badges over their left breast.

Right: Brigadier General William N. Gilmore (right) pins the bronze star medal on Captain Ralph Levine. Captain Levine has decorated his M1 helmet with the insignia of the 92d Armored Field Artillery Battalion, a red devil on a white background. The use of unit insignia on helmets and liners was far more prevalent during the Korean War than it had been during World War II.

Left: Corporal S. L. Spasser enjoys some reading material at an improvised library near the front lines. These libraries provided a welcome break to the monotony of life at the front. Spasser is wearing the third pattern HBT trousers, with bellows pockets on each thigh. Just visible underneath his HBT jacket is an issue white t-shirt.

Left: Lieutenant General William M. Hoge fires one of the 92d Armored Field Artillery Battalion's 155mm howitzers toward enemy lines. Hoge has his rank (three stars) and IX corps insignia stenciled on the front of his helmet. The massive 155mm could fire its rounds at targets more than 23 kilometers away.

Right: Two soldiers behind a berm provide cover fire as their comrades move forward. The man in the foreground is wearing the reversible parka's pile liner, made of imitation sheepskin with a blanket wool piece across the shoulders. He is carrying all of the ammunition for his M1 Garand rifle in a disposable bandolier, which could hold 48 rounds, worn over his shoulder.

Below: An infantry squad receives instructions from the squad leader during operations in February 1951. These men are all carrying improvised bedrolls over their shoulders. The G.I. at center also carries an extra ammunition bag. All wear leather and rubber shoepacs to help combat the cold.

Above: Members of the 25th Infantry Division enter the walled city of Suwon during the winter of 1951. The crew of the Sherman tank has festooned its vehicle with a variety of extra equipment intended to provide a few additional comforts: a common practice.

Below: Members of the 24th Infantry Division move their recoilless rifle to a position where they can support the attack of their fellow infantrymen. Several men carry additional ammunition for the rifle. The rounds were packaged in disposable cardboard tubes.

Above: The 7th RCT rear area in Sinpyoun-ni, Korea. Tent cities such as this were set up behind the lines to provide infantrymen with a place to rest and recoup. Many of these tents would be equipped with stoves and set up as warming tents.

Right: The camp for a heavy mortar company near Punggi, Korea. The photograph illustrates the extremely rugged terrain where much of the fighting in the peninsula took place. The 4.2-inch mortar's position is visible in the foreground. Behind the gun pit, additional mortar rounds are stacked in their cardboard tubes.

Left: Left to right: Captain Danials and Colonel Boswill confer with the commander of the 3d Infantry Division, Major General Robert Soule. Danials and Soule are both wearing World War II M1943 pile field caps while Boswill is wearing an M1943 field cap. As was customary, these officers have attached their rank insignia to the front of their caps.

Below: The crew of an M2-HB .50-caliber machine gun fires on enemy positions in the hills of Korea. The firepower of the .50-caliber machine gun made it ideal for firing on enemy troop formations and positions but its weight, 128 lb with the M3 tripod mount, made it difficult to move quickly.

Right: Major General John Church leaves Korea for Fort Benning, Georgia. Church is wearing the wool serge jacket and trousers. Commonly referred to as the 'Ike' jacket, after General Dwight D. Eisenhower, the Korean War version of this jacket was made of OD shade 33 wool serge, with no buttons at the wrist (unlike the World War II jacket).

Below right: A group of men from the 24th Infantry Division warms cans of C-Rations over a small fire. All but one are wearing the M1943 pile field cap, which featured pile lining on all flaps. The man seated at center is wearing the M1951 pile field cap, which did not have pile lining on the front visor.

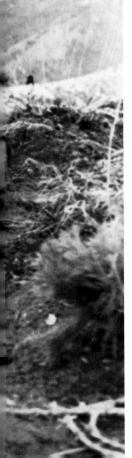

Above: Officers and men of the 1st Artillery after an awards ceremony. All of the men are wearing the pile field caps. The officers have attached their rank insignia to the front of their caps. The officers at front are all carrying .45-caliber pistols in leather M1916 holsters, which are attached to the right side of their M1936 pistol belts. These belts also have magazine pouches attached to the left side of the belt and first aid packets attached to the right.

Left: Sherman tanks carry ROK infantrymen into the line. The tank at the rear is carrying a Confederate flag from its radio antenna. Note the cans of .50-caliber ammunition that are carried on bustle racks at the rear of both tanks.

Right: General George Barber grimaces for the camera. He is wearing a World War II winter combat jacket, more popularly known as the 'tanker' jacket (but rarely worn in Korea), with World War II HBT fatigue trousers. Visible on the collars of his wool shirt is his rank insignia. He carries his .45-caliber pistol in an M-3 shoulder holster.

Below: Members of the 7th Infantry Division return fire on enemy positions. The man in the foreground is wearing a pair of two-buckle combat service boots. First issued in 1943, the two-buckle boots continued to be worn during the Korean War.

Left: Soldiers receive bronze stars for service in Korea. The man receiving his medal is wearing a World War II fatigue shirt. The enlisted men are all wearing the M1943 pile cap, while the general appears to be wearing the earlier lamb's wool winter cap. The flaps of the pile cap could be turned down for warmth.

Center left: A squad from the 2d Infantry Division moves up to the line. These men present a fairly typical appearance of infantrymen during combat operations, and are all wearing a variety of coats and jackets. While the man at the left front has an M1943 field jacket, the man second from left wears the World War II reversible parka. The man leading the column on the right has an improvised bedroll slung across his chest.

Bottom left: Members of the 2d Infantry Division pose in front of their jeeps. Note the lack of all insignia on their combat uniforms, with the exception of stripes on the sleeves of the non commissioned officers (NCOs). Although similarly uniformed and equipped, some of the men have slipped the elasticized olive drab camouflage helmet band around their helmets. The soldier seated second from the right has also obtained a pair of the M1944 goggles to protect his eyes from dust and debris while riding in his jeep.

Two crewmen of a 105mm howitzer rest while their comrades fire the gun. The tread pattern on the rubber sole of the combat service shoe is clear in the picture. The man standing behind the gun is wearing what appears to be a pair of rubberized wet weather trousers over his field uniform.

Above: A battery of 105mm howitzers fires on enemy positions. Note that the guns are all separated from each other. The rapid rate of fire has made it necessary for two of the guns' towing vehicles to come up behind the weapons with additional ammunition.

Below: Mortarmen prepare to fire their weapon. Both men are wearing the M1951 pile cap. The man on the left is also wearing an olive green (OG) shade 108 wool field shirt. Although ideally suited for the freezing conditions in Korea, the heavy wool field shirt was never received in sufficient quantities to be issued to all the soldiers who needed one.

Above: An M75 armored personnel carrier travels at night. Although in production during the war in Korea, the M75 was held back in anticipation of possible deployment to Europe.

Below: Two 155mm self-propelled howitzers are made ready to fire. Just visible at the rear of the M40 motor carriage is the blade that was lowered to stabilize the gun when firing. All of the artillerymen wear the M1943 uniform.

Above: G.I.s move into position. All are armed with M-2 carbines. Unlike the earlier M-1, the M-2 could fire in either automatic or semi-automatic mode. The officer at the front of the column has pinned rank insignia to the collar of his fatigue jacket.

Below: Officers in World War II fatigue uniforms confer during operations. The jackets of the general second from left and the major at right both have the internal gas-flap buttoned over the opening of their jackets. These gas-flaps were uncomfortable and were frequently removed from the inside of the shirt.

Above: A 105mm howitzer crew prepares to fire on the enemy. All of the members of this gun crew are wearing shoepacs. Referred to as 'swampers' by soldiers in Korea, the leather upper and rubber-bottomed shoepacs were intended to provide some warmth to G.I.s operating in winter conditions. Unfortunately, they proved inadequate for Korea's brutal winters.

Below: African American G.I.s fall in for an address by their commanding officer. All wear pile caps with field jackets and the M43 cotton over-trousers. Made of the same material as the field jacket, these were worn over wool service trousers.

Above: Infantrymen prepare to fire their M20 recoilless rifle at the enemy. The M20 was used for close support of infantrymen. Although heavy, at 118 lb, the M20 could be transported by a group of men and its 75mm shells proved highly effective against enemy targets.

Left: Soldiers of the 2d Infantry Division are transported to the front in an M39 armored utility vehicle. Developed at the end of World War II, the M39 saw extensive use in Korea.

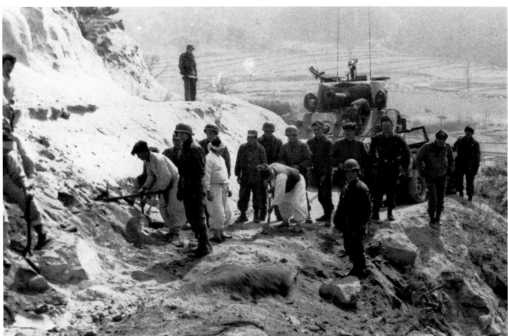

Above: American and ROK troops look on as South Korean civilians work to repair damage to a road. The men are all wearing M1943 combat clothing. A 2d Infantry Division insignia is visible on the shoulder of the man at front.

Below: G.I.s evacuate a wounded comrade. Rapid evacuation from the battlefield greatly increased the chance of survival. The man at right has attached a Mk II fragmentation grenade (left) and a Mk I illumination grenade to the pockets of his field jacket. Grenades were very useful during close trench fighting.

Above: Members of the 187th RCT (Airborne), the 'Rakasans,' board a C-119 prior to a practice jump. They are all wearing the T7A troop personnel parachutes over their M43 combat uniforms. Of special interest is the fact that most of these men are wearing the paratrooper's coveted jump boots rather than the more common two-buckle service shoe.

Below: Rakasans wait for their C-119 to take off prior to a practice jump. Although never employed in the numbers that they had been in World War II, paratroopers did make two combat jumps during the Korean War. Note the chaplain's insignia painted on the helmet of the trooper seated second from the right.

Above: G.I.s huddle on an M39 before moving to the front. For additional warmth, several of these men have lifted the hoods of their parkas or lowered the earflaps on their pile caps. The man seated at right with a pipe is wearing combat service boots, which only ever reached Korea in limited numbers. The service boot closely resembled the paratrooper jump boot but lacked a beveled heel.

Right: The crew of an M4 tank assigned to the 25th Infantry Division stops while a photographer snaps a picture. Two of the crewmen seated on the tank are wearing air force M5 protective helmets with the earflaps removed. Originally designed for aircrews so that they could wear the helmet over their flying helmets, the M5 saw some use among the armored personnel in Korea because it provided a degree of ballistic protection missing in the standard tanker's helmet.

Above: A 90mm gun of the 92d Armored Field Artillery position. Once the war of movement had ended, both sides constructed elaborate bunkers and fortifications reminiscent of World War I. The intricacy of this position indicates that the crew planned to remain at this location for some time.

Left: First Lieutenant Joseph Diran searches for targets with a B.C. scope. Diran has sewn the red and white Eighth Army insignia to the left shoulder of his fatigue shirt, which has been modified by the addition of pencil holders. He is also wearing his fatigue trousers bloused over the combat service boot.

Above: Members of the 92d Armored Field Artillery prepare to fire a round from one of their 90mm guns. The man ramming the shell into the breach is wearing the olive drab shade 31, stand-up collar (SUC) wool flannel shirt. The SUC shirt was introduced in 1947 to replace the wool shirt worn during World War II.

Above right: Sergeant Ray Boucher of the 92d AFA Battalion smiles for the camera. He has stenciled his helmet with his unit's red devil insignia. He is also wearing a Korean-manufactured red ascot with unit insignia embroidered to the front. Such unofficial paraphernalia was often worn to increase esprit de corps.

Right: Two officers of the 92d AFA salute during a retirement ceremony. The officer at right has sewn a nametape to the left breast of his field jacket. White nametapes first began to be worn in Korea, and were quite common although not universal. Both of these men have obtained leather glove shells, which were worn with wool knit inserts.

Left: A recoilless rifle crew prepares to fire its weapon. The rifle's peculiar honeycomb round is visible in the hands of the man at right. The man at left sighting the piece is wearing the OG107 sateen utility trousers that began to replace the HBT utility uniform toward the second half of the Korean War.

Left: Anna M. Rosenberg, the assistant secretary of defense, talks to members of the 45th Infantry Division during a visit to Korea. The men standing at right are wearing the M1946 pattern HBT jacket, which featured patch pockets and plastic buttons. Several of these men have attached their combat infantry badges to the left breast of their jackets.

Left: Officers of the 24th Infantry Division (left) turn over their positions to artillerymen of the 40th Infantry Division. The gunners from the 40th Division are all wearing M1948 parka shells with fur collars. They have crossed cannon insignia painted on their helmet liners. The officers at left are wearing a variety of outerwear including a field overcoat (left) and a parka type overcoat (center).

Gunners from the 40th Infantry Division clean the breach of their artillery piece. Both are wearing pile field caps underneath their M1 helmets. The man at right has the 40th Division insignia sewn to the left sleeve of his field jacket. The men are wearing the new OG107 sateen utility trousers.

Above: Members of the 224th Infantry Regiment, 40th Infantry Division, move up during the winter of 1952. They wear a variety of parkas and cold weather gear over their field jackets. All of these infantrymen are wearing pile caps underneath their M-1 helmets. Sergeant's insignia is painted on the front of several of the helmets. By this point in the war, more adequate winter clothing was beginning to be received by men in Korea.

Below: A 105mm gun fires on Chinese positions in Korea. The men are all wearing World War II fatigue jackets with later pattern OG107 utility trousers. The man with the shell, second from left, is wearing a white cotton t-shirt under his jacket. Empty storage tubes are around the gun, with extra rounds stacked on the right.

Above: Actor William Holden visits two officers from the 45th Infantry Division. The officer at the right is wearing the OG107 sateen utility jacket with rank and unit insignia. As was the fashion during the Korean War, both men are wearing their shirts tucked into their trousers.

Left: G.I.s prepare to go to the front line. The men are wearing their M1945 combat field pack with attached horseshoe rolls on their back. The horseshoe roll contained the soldier's blanket, tent poles, pegs and shelter half. The pack had been inspired by the United States Marine Corps' 782-web equipment.

Above: A 155mm battery of the 2d Infantry Division in position in 1952. Judging from the lack of more thorough defensive positions, this battery does not fear enemy counter-battery fire.

Below: The band of the 2d Infantry Division, including bagpipers, performs for Major General E.E. Partridge on October 1950. The pipers were unofficial members of the division band. They are wearing tartan kilts with sporrans and glengarries. Their 'doublets' are constructed from converted khaki cotton service shirts.

Above: An M26 Pershing tank fires on Chinese positions. The M26 had originally been developed to combat heavier German tanks during World War II. Although the war ended before the M26 could make a significant contribution to Allied victory, it was effective in Korea against Communist T-34 tanks. The crewman at left is wearing the fiber-armored crewman's helmet.

Right: Infantrymen pinned down by enemy fire take shelter behind a Korean building. Five of the men are wearing the venerable M1 helmet. As was most common in Korea, the helmet is worn without a helmet net. Two of the men are wearing the HBT mechanic's cap.

Above: G.I.s trudge down from the Korean hills. The man at the center is wearing the M1943 field cap. Intended to replace the HBT mechanic's cap and the World War II wool jeep cap, the M43 field cap was made of the same material as the M43 jacket and trousers.

Left: Officers of the 45th Infantry Division on board the transport ship taking them to Korea. The officers are all wearing the khaki shade tropical worsted wool service shirts and trousers with OD51 necktie and worsted wool service cap. The officer at the front is wearing green combat leader's tabs on the epaulettes of his shirt.

Opposite page, top: A column of M26 tanks rests prior to moving into action. When not in combat, the turret of the Pershing tank was turned around and secured facing rearward. Each of these tanks has extra sections of tread for their vehicle attached to the side of the turret.

Opposite page, bottom: Members of the 45th Infantry Division's 180th Infantry Regiment pose for a group photo in 1952. These men have been fortunate enough to receive the M1951 parka and pile caps. The officers and NCOs have affixed their rank insignia to the front of their caps.

Above: A forward observer keeps watch for enemy movements. He is kneeling behind a stack of .30-caliber ammunition cans. At his side is an SCR300 radio. Just visible on his left shoulder is his sergeant's insignia. This smaller insignia, which featured blue stripes on a yellow background, was unique to the Korean War.

Below: Three soldiers provide covering fire for the operator of an M2-2 flamethrower. Although the flamethrower was effective against enemy positions, the operators were vulnerable to enemy fire and would generally only approach enemy positions with support from other G.I.s.

Above: Tank crewmen prepare their vehicles for action. The men are all wearing M1943 combat uniform with pile caps and rubber overshoes. Slung to the side of the turret of the tank in the foreground are the M1945 packs of the vehicle's crewmen.

Below: Weary G.I.s enjoy a hot meal. They are eating out of their two-piece 'meat can' mess tins and drinking out of canteen cups. The meat can and canteen cups were little changed since first introduction in 1910.

Left: Two Sherman M4A3E8 tanks travel along a road in Korea. Both are festooned with miscellaneous equipment.

Opposite page: The crew of an M-24 light tank guards a roadblock on the Naktong River. The crewman sitting on the ground is wearing a pair of World War II reverse upper service shoes. Although these boots had been discontinued by the time of the Korean War, stocks remaining in Japan meant that they were occasionally worn in Korea.

Below: Soldiers on board a troopship wait to set sail. They wear a variety of uniforms, including the khaki cotton service uniform (as worn by the man standing near the 'fire station' stencil), which was worn infrequently in Korea.

Above: Members of the 38th Infantry Regiment pose for a picture after an awards ceremony. Most of these men are wearing World War II fatigues but have tucked their shirts into their trousers in the Korean War fashion. The man kneeling third from the left in the front row has an M2 flash hider affixed to the muzzle of his M1 Garand, indicating that he is armed with the M1D Garand sniper rifle.

Below: The crew of a .50-caliber machine gun stays alert as armored vehicles move out in front of them. The man at left has attached an M-4 bayonet to his M-2 carbine. Although the early models could not accommodate a bayonet, from 1944 carbines were fitted with a bayonet lug. In Korea, most carbines featured this attachment.

Right: The crew of a water-cooled .30-caliber machine gun supports an infantry attack. The man nearest to the camera has added some padding to the top of his M1 helmet. Affixed to the back of his pistol belt is the cover for his M1943 folding entrenching tool.

Below: Artillerymen pose for a picture. The men sitting on the gun's tail are wearing a variety of footwear including, from left to right, shoepacs, reverse upper service shoes, two-buckle boots and combat service boots. The men are also wearing a variety of field clothing, including, on the man seated second from right, an OG107 sateen utility shirt.

Opposite page, top: The Eighth Army Corps band greets troops arriving in Korea. The bandsmen wear early pattern HBT fatigues, and have the Corps' insignia stenciled to the right side of their helmet liners. Interestingly, the bandsman playing fourth from the right has brought his M-2 carbine with him to the performance.

Opposite page, bottom: Signalmen of the 2d Infantry Division repair damaged lines. They are wearing fiber helmet liners. The man kneeling second from the right is testing his repaired line with an EE8B field telephone. A .30-caliber machine gun is attached to the front passenger side of their jeep.

Above: Members of the 37th Field Artillery dig in near the front lines. Warming tents for the crewmen have been set up in front of the guns' positions. Additional ammunition has been stacked outside of the gun pits.

Below: An M19 'Duster' searches for enemy positions. The Duster was a lightly armored anti-aircraft vehicle featuring the twin 40mm Bofors cannon and, in this case, an additional .50-caliber machine gun. Although used against Communist aircraft, the Duster was also effective as a ground support weapon.

Above: Men of the 2d Infantry Division's 2d Reconnaissance Honor Guard pose for a picture. They are all wearing field jackets with divisional insignia attached, and rayon ascots in branch-of-service color.

Below: A 105mm howitzer of the 2d Infantry Division fires on enemy positions. These guns have been set up behind a wall of sandbags.

Above: Military Policemen (MPs) of the 2d Infantry Division search a suspected North Korean soldier. Two of them wear helmets stenciled with a red band and white MP letters. The MP at right is wearing the dark blue and white MP brassard, while the MP squatting at left is wearing a similar brassard but with the letters in Korean. ·

Below: Members of the 45th Infantry Division pose for a picture. Many of these men are wearing commercially manufactured 'Ridgway' caps. The Ridgway cap was, essentially, an M43 cap with a stiffener inserted into it. Kneeling in the front row (fourth from left) is this group's medic, distinguished by his white brassard with Red Cross.

Opposite page, top: A troopship arrives at Yokahama, Japan. Troopships such as this were necessary to transport the huge numbers of men and materiel to Korea from Japan and the United States. The long supply line greatly complicated efforts to provide adequately for G.I.s in Korea.

Opposite page, bottom: American and ROK troops are transported to the front on the back of an M26 Pershing tank. These were frequently used to transport G.I.s to the front lines. Once the vehicle got within range of enemy small arms, the men would dismount and advance on foot.

Above: Members of the 40th Infantry Division leave Japan, bound for Korea. These men wear wool shirts with M43 caps and trousers. Several are also wearing five-button high-neck sweaters. One of the men wears the helmet liner for his M1 helmet, with his divisional insignia stenciled to the side.

Above: A color guard from the 92d Armored Field Artillery Battalion begins an awards ceremony. The men wear a variety of fatigue uniforms and rank insignia. All of their helmets, however, have been stenciled with the unit's devil insignia. The colors are, from left to right, national colors, regimental standard, and unofficial battery colors.

Left: Lieutenant Colonel Duff Green of the 73d Tank Battalion smiles after an award ceremony. He leans on the front glacis of a Pershing tank decorated with the face of a tiger, which the G.I.s believed would frighten the superstitious Chinese troops.

Opposite page, top: An M26 tank crew keeps watch for enemy movement. These tankers have dug in their vehicle to reduce the tank's silhouette. The men wear parkas and armored crewman's helmets.

Opposite page, bottom: The crew of a Pershing tank loads 90mm rounds into its vehicle. In addition to its other armament, the Pershing could carry up to 70 rounds of ammunition for its main gun.

Left: Members of the 2d Infantry Division receive decorations from a X Corps officer. All of the award recipients have their divisional insignia attached to the left sleeve of their fatigue jacket.

Below: Two tank cewmen work on the road wheels of their M26 Pershing tank. Both wear the second pattern HBT mechanic's cap with the long bill.